Y0-DJQ-267

A new boy named Ben has a big problem at school.

Reading Vocabulary Words

attendance
mumbled
sugarcane

High-Frequency Words

story	*didn't*
big	*filled*
kid	*look*
page	*like*

Building Future Vocabulary

* These vocabulary words do not appear in this text. They are provided to develop related oral vocabulary that first appears in future texts.

Words:	*background*	*submit*	*secure*
Levels:	Library	Library	Library

Comprehension Strategy

Forming and supporting opinions

Fluency Skill

Using loudness and softness to express emotion

Phonics Skill

Developing and applying knowledge of vowel digraph *ea* (pl<u>ea</u>se, t<u>ea</u>cher, r<u>ea</u>son, <u>ea</u>sy, s<u>ea</u>, m<u>ea</u>n)

Reading-Writing Connection

Writing a paragraph

Home Connection

Send home one of the Flying Colors Take-Home books for children to share with their families.

Differentiated Instruction

Before reading the text, query children to discover their level of understanding of the comprehension strategy — Forming and supporting opinions. As you work together, provide additional support to children who show a beginning mastery of the strategy.

Focus on ELL

- Have children turn to the illustration of sugarcane on page 9. Have children tell what they know about sugar. Ask them what a cane looks like. Point out that sugar comes from sugarcane, a plant that grows straight like a cane.

- Ask children to name foods that are sweetened with sugar.

Using This Teaching Version

1. Before Reading

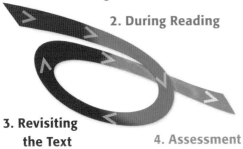

2. During Reading

3. Revisiting the Text

4. Assessment

This Teaching Version will assist you in directing children through the process of reading.

1. **Begin with Before Reading** to familiarize children with the book's content. Select the skills and strategies that meet the needs of your children.

2. Next, go to During Reading to help children become familiar with the text, and then to read individually on their own.

3. **Then, go back to Revisiting the Text** and select those specific activities that meet children's needs.

4. Finally, finish with Assessment to confirm children are ready to move forward to the next text.

Building Background

- Write *attendance* on the board. Read it aloud. Ask children to name places that people attend and list their responses on the board.

- Introduce the book by reading the title, talking about the cover illustration, and sharing the overview.

Building Future Vocabulary
Use Interactive Modeling Card: Word Game

- Write *secure* in the first box of the Word Game. Have children think of words that rhyme with *secure* and enter them in the second box. Use the third box to make new words from *secure*.

- Add prefixes, suffixes, or inflected endings in the fourth box. Write synonyms in the fifth box.

- In the sixth box, write *secure* in a sentence using at least five words. Use the last box to record the total number of words.

Introduction to Reading Vocabulary

- On blank cards write: attendance, mumbled, and sugarcane. Read them aloud. Tell children these words will appear in the text of *Ben's Story.*

- Use each word in a sentence for understanding.

Introduction to Comprehension Strategy

- Explain that as you read a story you can form opinions, or ideas, about what you read, and you can support these opinions with facts from the story.

- Tell children they will be stopping at different points in the story to form opinions about what has happened so far. Explain that they will also be supporting their opinions with story events.

- Using the front and back covers, ask children if they think the illustrations give clues about the title. Have them support their opinions with details from the illustrations.

Introduction to Phonics

- List on the board: **please, teacher, reason, easy, sea,** and **mean.** Read each word aloud and use it in a sentence. Point out that all of the words have the vowel digraph *ea* and form the long *e* sound, while the *a* is silent. Circle the *ea* in each word and use each word in a sentence.

- Ask children for more examples of words with vowel digraph *ea*. Write the words on the board and have children circle the *ea* in each word.

Modeling Fluency

- Read the second paragraph on page 4 aloud, modeling the use of loudness to express the children's frustration.

- Point out that the quotation marks signal that a character is speaking. Talk about the exclamation points and the emotions they convey.

2 During Reading

Book Talk
Beginning on page T4, use the During Reading notes on the left-hand side to engage children in a book talk. On page 16, follow with Individual Reading.

During Reading

Book Talk

- Explain to children that the illustrations on the cover and title page help readers form opinions about the story.

- **Comprehension Strategy**
  Point out the table of contents and discuss with children how the chapter titles give clues about parts of the story. Ask *Which chapter sounds the most interesting? Why?*

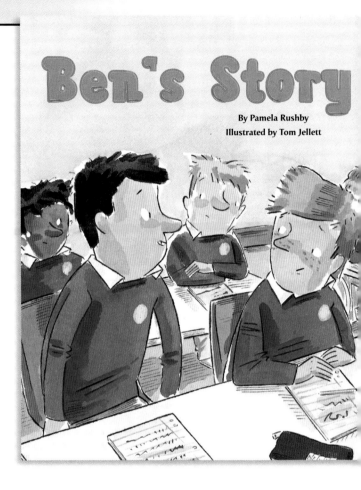

Turn to page 2 – Book Talk

Ben's Story

By Pamela Rushby

Illustrated by Tom Jellett

Future Vocabulary

- Say *The five chapter titles give you some* background *knowledge of the story.* Background means important information. Discuss what children know about the story based on the chapter titles.

Now revisit pages 2–3

During Reading

Book Talk

- Have children locate the word mumbled on page 2.

- **Comprehension Strategy** Say *In the text, you will read that Ben* mumbled *his greeting to the class. Why do you think Ben did not give a cheerful reply?* (The chapter title is "A Problem." His problem might be making him sad.)

- Discuss with children times when they mumbled and why.

Turn to page 4 – Book Talk

Chapter 1

A Problem

When I started at this new school, I knew they'd find out about me. I didn't expect it'd be on the very first day, but it was.

The teacher, Mr. Lee, introduced me. "This is Ben," he said. "I know you'll make him feel welcome."

"Hi, Ben," everyone said cheerfully.

"Hi," I mumbled. I didn't expect to be here long enough to make friends.

2

"Now, where shall we put you?" Mr. Lee said. "Ah, next to Jon, I think. You'll look after Ben, won't you, Jon?"

The kid called Jon said, "Sure," and grinned, but I didn't smile back.

I sat down and looked around the room. It didn't look much different than all the other classrooms I'd been in, and I'd been in a lot of classrooms.

My family moves around a lot, so I've been to ten different schools, and I'm only nine. Maybe that was the reason I had a problem – a big problem.

3

Future Vocabulary

• Say Background *has other meanings too. For example, your* background *is the way you are raised. How might Ben's* background *be different from the other children's?* (Ben's dad is a truck driver, so they move often. Most children have not gone to ten schools by the time they are nine years old.)

Now revisit pages 4–5

3

During Reading

Book Talk

- **Phonics Skill** Have children locate words with vowel digraph *ea. (each, please, least)* Point out the location of *ea* in each of the words.

- Have children locate the word *attendance* on page 4. Explain that *attendance* is a form of *attend*, which means to be present.

- **Comprehension Strategy** Ask *Why do you think Mr. Lee has to take* attendance*?* (The class is starting, and he wants to see who is present and who is not.)

- Have children talk about events that may have a large attendance. (sporting events, concerts, movies)

Turn to page 6 — Book Talk

What I Did on My Vacation

Mr. Lee took attendance. Then he handed out paper and pencils and wrote something on the whiteboard. "There you go," he said. "Two pages from each of you, please, before lunch."

The class groaned. "Not 'What I Did on My Vacation,' Mr. Lee!" they protested. "Not again!"

Mr. Lee grinned. "At least you'll all have something to write about," he said. "You all did *something* during the summer!"

The class groaned again, but they all started working. I picked up my pencil and tried to look as if I was thinking.

4

4

Future Vocabulary

- Say *Mr. Lee's students submit to his decision to write about their summer vacation even though they do not want to do it again.* Submit *means to obey or follow.*

- Discuss with children when it is important for people to submit to someone or something because it is the right thing to do. (obeying laws to protect them, following a decision or vote of the majority of people)

Now revisit pages 6–7

Beside me that Jon kid was writing away. I couldn't believe it – he'd filled half a page already.

Mr. Lee walked around the room. He stopped beside me and said, "Not started yet, Ben?"

5

During Reading

Book Talk

- **Comprehension Strategy** Ask *Why does Ben think Jon is showing off?* (Jon has written a whole page.) *Do you agree with Ben? What is your opinion of Jon?*

Turn to page 8 – Book Talk

"No," I said.

"So what did you do during the summer?" Mr. Lee asked.

"Nothing much," I said. "Well, I went on five trips with my dad."

"*Five trips?*" said Mr. Lee. "That's a lot of traveling."

"My dad drives trucks," I said. "I go along with him for company."

"You could write about that, couldn't you?" said Mr. Lee.

"Yeah," I said. "I guess I could."

"Get started then," said Mr. Lee, and he walked away.

6

I could see that Jon kid looking at me, and I could also see he'd written a whole page.

"Show off!" I thought.

Future Vocabulary

- Explain that *secure* is another word for confident. Ask children to name a sport or hobby in which they feel secure in participating. Ask *How can you tell that Jon feels secure about his writing?* (He has already written a whole page; writing is easy for him.)

Now revisit pages 8–9

During Reading

Book Talk

- Have children find the word *sugarcane* on page 9.

- Ask *What is Mr. Lee doing in the illustration to show that he is interested in Ben's story?* (leaning forward, listening, looking directly at Ben).

- **Comprehension Strategy** Say *Ben tells Mr. Lee about all sorts of big things he has seen on the road. Which do you think is the most unusual? Why?*

Turn to page 10 – Book Talk

Chapter 3

Big Things

Mr. Lee walked by again and said, "Still no inspiration, Ben?"

I shook my head.

"Tell me about the things you see on the road," Mr. Lee said. "What do you like best?"

That was easy! "I like the big things," I said.

"Big things?" said Mr. Lee.

"Yes," I said. "There's a Big Banana and a Big Shrimp and a Big Cow and a Big Pineapple. They're cool." I told Mr. Lee all about them – how you could go inside the Big Cow and climb all the way to the top of the Big Pineapple.

"Great!" said Mr. Lee. "Write about big things, then!"

8

Revisiting the Text

I started to write. I wrote two lines. Then I looked at them and erased some words. I turned my back to stop that Jon kid from looking at my writing. He was up to three pages.

When Mr. Lee came back, I'd still only written two lines, and I could tell he was getting annoyed with me. "Better get busy, Ben," he said. "If the big things are no good, write about the places you like best. What are they?"

"I like one place where there are hills covered with sugarcane," I said. "The sugarcane runs right down to the sea. The wind blows through the sugarcane, making it move like waves in a sea. Only it's a green sea, not a blue one."

9

metaphor

Future Vocabulary

- Point to the sugarcane fields in the background of the illustration on page 9. Say *Look at the sugarcane fields in the background of the illustration. Are sugarcane fields really behind Ben and Mr. Lee?* (no) *How do you know they are not really there?* (The fields are in a thought cloud. The illustrator is showing us what Ben is talking about.)

Now revisit pages 10–11

simile

During Reading

Book Talk

- **Fluency Skill** Have volunteers take turns reading the first paragraph on page 11. Remind them to read Mr. Lee's dialogue with expression.

- **Phonics Skill** Have children locate the words with vowel digraph *ea. (read, reading)* Point out that *read* has a short e sound when the word is used in the past tense, such as "Last week I read two books."

Turn to page 12 – Book Talk

"Yes?" said Mr. Lee.

"And I like the rain forest," I said. "It's all cool and dim and musty smelling, and the trees stretch up so high you can't see the sky."

"Excellent!" said Mr. Lee. "Beautiful words! Write them down, Ben."

But I didn't. I just sat, and that Jon kid kept writing and writing and writing – making me look bad!

I thought, "I'll get you at lunchtime!"

10

Revisiting the Text

Chapter 4
Ben's Story

"Time to finish up," Mr. Lee called out. "There's just time to read a few stories out loud before lunch. Do I have any volunteers?" He stopped by me and looked at the two messy, rubbed-out lines I'd written.

"Hmmm," he said. "There's a problem, isn't there, Ben?" I didn't say anything. "You've got a problem with writing," he said quietly. "That's nothing to be worried about. We can fix it. What about your reading — how's that?"

"Not too good," I mumbled.

"We can fix that, too," Mr. Lee said, "just as long as we know. It'll be OK. I'll talk to you later."

11

Future Vocabulary

- Say *Ben describes the way the trees stretch up high in the rain forest. The trees block out sunlight and make the rain forest dark. Would you feel secure in a dark forest? In other words, would you feel safe?*

- Ask *What makes you feel secure?* If necessary, prompt children with questions about their family or a favorite stuffed animal.

Now revisit pages 12–13

I'd = I had

During Reading

- **Comprehension Strategy** Ask *Do you think Jon is making fun of Ben? What does Mr. Lee do that gives us a clue that Jon is nice?* (He looks carefully at Jon's writing and smiles. Then he gives him permission to read it aloud.)

- **Phonics Skill** Have children locate words with vowel digraph *ea. (read, mean)* Point out that in this story *mean* has to do with understanding something. Explain that *mean* is also another word for cruel. For example, Ben thinks Jon is being mean to him.

Turn to page 14 – Book Talk

I just knew that Jon kid had heard every word. He knew I couldn't read or write properly! I was *really* going to get him at lunchtime!

"Who'd like to read their stories out loud?" Mr. Lee asked.

A few kids put up their hands, but Jon's was up first. "Can I read Ben's story, Mr. Lee?" he called out.

I stared at him. What did he mean, my story? There was no "my story" – well, only two lines of it. Was that Jon kid making fun of me?

"Show me what you mean, Jon," said Mr. Lee.

12

Future Vocabulary
• Say *Jon and the others are raising their hands. They are trying to* secure *Mr. Lee's attention.* Secure *means to get hold of.* Discuss with children other ways people try to secure someone's attention. (waving, talking, shouting, snapping fingers)

Now revisit pages 14–15

Jon showed Mr. Lee what he'd been writing. There were five pages at least. Mr. Lee looked carefully at it. Then he smiled and said, "Go ahead, Jon."

I slid down in my chair. That Jon kid was in *big* trouble at lunchtime!

13

During Reading

Book Talk

- **Comprehension Strategy**
  Review children's opinions about Jon. Say *The five chapter titles give you some background knowledge of the story.* Background *means important information.* Discuss what children know about the story based on the chapter titles. (Ben thinks Jon is nice and may become a friend.) Have children share a time when they formed an opinion about someone before getting to know them.

Turn to page 16 – Book Talk

Then Jon started to speak. "I wrote Ben's story down," he said, "just the way he told it because it was really good." He cleared his throat. "Ben's Story," he read. "I like the Big Things – they're cool! You can go right inside the Big Cow. You can climb right to the top of the Big Pineapple . . . "

He kept reading – about the way the sugarcane fields look like a green sea and the way the rain forest is cool and dim and so thick you can't see the sky. When he'd finished, everyone was quiet.

14

"Beautiful words," said Mr. Lee at last. "I think that should be printed in the school newsletter. You're a real writer, Ben!"

"A writer?" I said. "But . . . but I can't . . . I mean . . . "

"Oh, *that!*" said Mr. Lee. "We'll soon fix that! Class – a round of applause for Ben's story!"

15

Future Vocabulary

- Say *Mr. Lee says Ben is a real writer. Ben seems surprised because he does not have a strong background, or training, in reading and writing. Why do you think Mr. Lee believes Ben is a real writer?* (Ben is a great storyteller; he uses beautiful words.)

- Say *Mr. Lee thinks Ben should submit, or turn in, his story to the school newsletter. Have you ever submitted a story or a picture for others to read or see?*

*Go to page T5 –
Revisiting the Text*

During Reading

Book Talk

- Leave this page for children to discover on their own when they read the book individually.

Individual Reading

Have each child read the entire book at his or her own pace while remaining in the group.

Go to page T5 —
Revisiting the Text

Chapter 5

Maybe . . .

Everyone clapped and smiled, and this time, I smiled back. When Jon sat down beside me, I smiled at him, too.

Maybe I was going to like this school. Maybe this time I'd make some friends. Maybe soon I wouldn't have a problem.

Lots of maybes, I thought, but one thing was for sure. I wasn't going to get Jon at lunchtime!

16

During independent work time, children can read the online book at: **www.rigbyflyingcolors.com**

Revisiting the Text

Future Vocabulary

- Use the notes on the right-hand pages to develop oral vocabulary that goes beyond the text. These vocabulary words first appear in future texts. These words are: *background*, *submit*, and *secure*.

  Turn back to page 1

Reading Vocabulary Review

Activity Sheet: Classifying New Words

- Have children write *mumbled* in the first column of the Classifying New Words chart. Tell them to use the word *mumbled* in a sentence.

- Ask children to decide whether *mumbled* is a noun, verb, adjective, or adverb. Monitor as they place a check mark in the appropriate column.

Comprehension Strategy Review

Use Interactive Modeling Card: Main Idea and Supporting Details

- Remind children that the main idea tells what the story is mostly about.

- Together, write the main idea on the tabletop. Then write four supporting details on the legs of the table.

Phonics Review

- On the board, write vowel digraph *ea* words from the story, such as *teacher*, *easy*, and *sea*.

- Have volunteers suggest *ea* digraph words to add to the list, such as *bean* and *each*. Sort the words by initial, medial, and final *ea* digraphs.

Fluency Review

- Have volunteers read aloud the parts of Ben and Mr. Lee on page 8, while you read the narration.

- Remind children to use loudness and softness to express the characters' emotions.

Reading-Writing Connection

Activity Sheet: Making Your Own Judgment

To assist children with linking reading and writing:

- Choose and write a story event in the first column of the Making Your Own Judgment chart. Write a judgment about the event and a fact to support the judgment in the second and third columns. Then have children use other story events to complete the chart.

- Have children write a paragraph about how this school may be different from Ben's other schools.

4 Assessment

Assessing Future Vocabulary

Work with each child individually. Ask questions that elicit each child's understanding of the Future Vocabulary words. Note each child's responses:

- Which place has more background noise, a classroom during a test or a playground during recess?
- What should you do to your writing before you submit a final copy?
- What can you do to make your house more secure?

Assessing Comprehension Strategy

Work with each child individually. Note each child's understanding of forming and supporting opinions:

- How did you feel about Jon at the beginning of the story? Why?
- Do you think moving around a lot is a good or bad thing? Explain.
- Do you think it was right for Jon to write down Ben's story?
- Why do you think reading and writing are important skills to have?

Assessing Phonics

Work with each child individually. Have each child turn to page 4 and identify the words with vowel digraph *ea. (each, please)* Have each child use the words in a sentence. Note each child's responses for understanding vowel digraph *ea*:

- Did each child accurately identify and read the vowel digraph *ea* words on the page?
- Did each child easily identify the vowel digraph *ea* in each word?
- Did each child use the word properly in a sentence?

Assessing Fluency

Have each child read page 11 to you. Note each child's understanding of using loudness and softness to express emotion:

- Was each child able to change from a louder voice to a softer voice when Mr. Lee speaks only to Ben?
- Was each child able to express Mr. Lee's emotion while whispering?

Interactive Modeling Cards

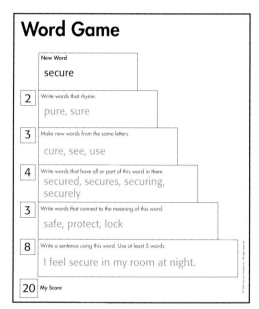

Word Game

	New Word	
	secure	
2	Write words that rhyme.	pure, sure
3	Make new words from the same letters.	cure, see, use
4	Write words that have all or part of this word in them.	secured, secures, securing, securely
3	Write words that connect to the meaning of this word.	safe, protect, lock
8	Write a sentence using this word. Use at least 5 words.	I feel secure in my room at night.
20	My Score	

Directions: With children, fill in the Word Game using the word *secure*.

Main Idea and Supporting Details

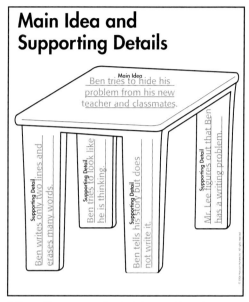

Main Idea: Ben tries to hide his problem from his new teacher and classmates.

Supporting Detail: Ben writes only two lines and erases many words.

Supporting Detail: Ben tries to look like he is thinking.

Supporting Detail: Ben tells his story but does not write it.

Supporting Detail: Mr. Lee figures out that Ben has a writing problem.

Directions: With children, fill in the Main Idea and Supporting Details chart for *Ben's Story*.

Discussion Questions

- Who is new at the school? (Literal)
- Why does Ben want to "get Jon" at lunchtime? (Critical Thinking)
- Why do you think Mr. Lee calls Ben a writer? (Inferential)

Activity Sheets

Classifying New Words

New Word	Noun (person, place, or thing)	Verb (action word)	Adjective or Adverb (describing word)
mumbled		X	

Making Your Own Judgment

Story Event or Nonfiction Fact	Judgment	Support for Judgment
Ben arrives at a new school.	Ben isn't used to keeping friends.	Ben's family moves often.

Directions: Have children fill in the Classifying New Words chart using the word *mumbled* and other new words from the story.

Directions: Have children fill in the Making Your Own Judgment chart for *Ben's Story*.

Optional: On a separate blank paper, have children write a paragraph telling why they think this school might be different from Ben's other schools.